THIS BOOK BELONGS TO:

_____

I have put it off long enough. I am ready to
get my shit together. Right here, right now.

If found, please ...

return

burn

sell

get your shit together
and buy your own
f*cking copy

D1041036

Also by Sarah Knight

The Life-Changing Magic of Not Giving a F*ck

Get Your Sh*t Together

You Do You

get

your

SH*T

together

JOURNAL

practical ways to cut the bullsh*t and win at life

sarah knight

Little, Brown and Company
New York   Boston   London

What it is

The *Get Your Sh*t Together Journal* is based on a book called *Get Your Sh*t Together: how to stop worrying about what you should do so you can finish what you need to do and start doing what you want to do.* The book told my personal story of going from depressed corporate cubicle dweller to drinking-piña-coladas-on-the-beach freelancer, as well as including many examples of getting one's shit together, and approximately 400 jokes and swear words. (Each.)

The journal is designed to be more portable and even more practical, covering the essentials of what I call "GYST theory" (more on that on page 41) and highlighting all my best tips and tricks for fast, easy reference on the go, but also providing plenty of space for you to write down your goals, tasks, appointments, hopes, dreams, and grocery lists.

You should also feel free to doodle. Doodling is fun.

If you've already read the book, then first off, thank you! Second, I think you'll find the journal a useful companion—if for no other reason than you'll get a second crack at the coloring exercise on page 72. If, however, this journal is your introduction to the entire concept of getting your shit together, then I hope it gets you off to a very good start indeed. And if you find yourself hooked on success and goal-achievement and winning at life, well, there's more where that came from.

Disclaimer

Despite the relative decrease in quantity of swear words from the original book, this journal is still chock-full of 'em. So please don't go in expecting sunshine and kittens and be upset when you're greeted with shitstorms and shittens. OK? Excellent.

Let's do
this shit

Who it's for

Do you work too much, play too little, and never have enough time to devote to the people and things that truly make you happy? Are you overburdened by responsibilities or exhausted, stressed out, anxious, maybe even panic-stricken by the commitments in your diary? Are you feeling life is all a bit too much — and very much like you don't have your shit together?

Congratulations! (Well, sort of.) This journal is for you.

But it will work in different ways for different people. So let's take a moment to figure out exactly in which ways your shit is lacking togetherness — by way of a cultural archetype known as Alvin and the Chipmunks.

First appearing on American television as *The Alvin Show* in 1961, these lovable singing rodents gained popularity through their 1983–87 cartoon *Alvin and the Chipmunks*, as well as subsequent globally released live-action films with sequels still being produced as of this writing. Quite the franchise.

Which chipmunk are you?

1. **Some words to describe myself:**
   a) I'm nice, agreeable, naive.
   b) I'm fun and talk a good game, but live life by the seat of my pants.
   c) I'm an industrious, successful overachiever who appears to have my shit together.

2. **My New Year's resolution should probably be:**
   a) Be on time. For once.
   b) Hit deadlines on purpose instead of by accident.
   c) Set some goddamn boundaries.

3. **My calendar:**
   a) Doesn't exist.
   b) Is in a drawer ... somewhere?
   c) Is so full I had to buy a second one.

4. **My motto:**
   a) "I don't even know where to start."
   b) "Fake it 'til you make it!"
   c) "Give it to me; I'll get it done."

5. **My work performance evaluation:**
   a) "She's not great at following directions."
   b) "She's cool, but I'm not always sure I can trust her."
   c) "She NAILS Excel spreadsheets."

6. When something stressful happens, my go-to move is to:
   a) Hide under the bed.
   b) Run away.
   c) Pop six Valium.

7. Where are my confidence levels these days?
   a) Hiding under the bed with me.
   b) Great—I got this.
   c) I have my ups and downs.

8. My biggest fear is:
   a) Do I have to pick one?
   b) That I'll never have enough money to retire.
   c) If I don't check my e-mail every hour the world will explode.

9. It's the first day of work after a long vacation:
   a) Oh, man. I didn't sleep last night because I was so anxious about coming back.
   b) I think I'm still drunk.
   c) What vacation? I was working the whole time.

10. Where will I be with my New Year's resolutions in a month?
    a) Sitting on the couch with a jar of Nutella and a spoon.
    b) Same place I am now.
    c) At least ten steps ahead of expectations—but also having a panic attack.

If you got mostly As … you're a Theodore.

The youngest of the performing chipmunk brothers, Theodore is a sweetheart, but also a bit clueless. You might say he's along for the ride, but never, ever in the driver's seat. Like Theodore, some people just can't get it together, period. Full stop. They're constantly spilling on themselves (and others), losing their (and other people's) possessions, and making life far more difficult for themselves (and everybody else) than it needs to be.

These are the folks—however nice and well-intentioned they may be—who are chronically late, underprepared, and overwhelmed. They have to open their suitcases at the airline check-in desk to take out two pairs of shoes, a souvenir mug, and a jar of beach sand that caused their bags to exceed the weight limit. Then they have to frantically figure out how to get this stuff on the plane before everybody in line behind them revolts. If you are a Theodore, fear not—you can get your shit *and* your luggage together.

Shit Theodores may need help getting together:

- Showing up on time
- Following directions
- Remembering where they put stuff
- Keeping their calendar up to date
- Actually owning a calendar

If you got mostly Bs ... you're an Alvin.

The eldest chipmunk is fun and he talks a good game, but he doesn't plan very far ahead, which frequently gets him into trouble. Alvin's kind of a "fake it 'til you make it" guy, where the ratio of *making it* to *not making it* is weighted toward the latter. When the going gets tough, it's usually his own damn fault—and he bails, initiating the exasperated "Alllllllllvin!!!" refrain from his adoptive human dad/manager, Dave. (They're a cartoon family. Don't overthink it.)

Alvins (the humans, not the chipmunks) skate by on the day-to-day stuff, but when it comes to doing shit on a larger scale, they falter. These people arrive home from a relatively productive day at work and make dinner in the microwave because the oven door has been broken for three months and they haven't gotten around to dealing with it. Or they can totally manage a fantasy football team, but when it comes to planning for retirement it's as though numbers and statistics cease to have meaning. Finally, Alvins make the rest of us—bosses, colleagues, friends, back-up singers, etc.—nervous that we can't depend on them. Eventually the chances run out, the opportunities dry up, and you're just another boy band casualty. It doesn't have to be this way.

If you Alvins have your shit together a little bit, you can get your shit together for the big stuff.

Shit Alvins may need help getting together:

- Hitting deadlines (on purpose)
- Sticking to a budget
- Sticking to a diet
- Event planning
- Planning anything more than a week in advance

If you got mostly Cs ... you're a Simon.

Finally, there's Simon. Middle sibling, chess wizard, rocks glasses and a blue turtleneck. Always prodding Theodore, cleaning up after Alvin and generally doing more for the family than Michael Corleone.

Simons are objectively industrious, successful, and know how to operate a suitcase. In their fully functional, chef's-quality ovens, they roast chickens on the regular. They plan elaborate shindigs, never say no to a friend in need, and are very, very good at spreadsheets. And PowerPoint. Other people marvel at Simons, whose grace under fire is complemented by their perfectly matched belts, shoes, and handbags.

Yeah, Simons' shit *seems* to be together ... but under the surface, maybe it's not. They may have perfected the illusion—operating under the mistaken belief that being in demand, booked-up, and perennially under the gun is a good thing—but their shit is on struggle mode even if nobody else can see it.

Shit Simons may need help getting together:

- Prioritizing
- Setting boundaries
- Ending a relationship
- Switching careers
- Maintaining their sanity

Whether you're an Alvin, a Simon, or a Theodore, remember this:

Get Your Shit Together is not an admonition — It's a rallying cry.

What does it mean?

Getting your shit together does not mean packing your calendar to the brim just for the sake of packing your calendar to the brim.

It does not mean sucking it up, doing everything on your to-do list, then doing everything on someone else's to-do list, and doing it yesterday.

And it does not mean sacrificing your mental and physical health to the cause.

What it DOES mean is managing your calendar and to-do list in such a way that the shit that needs doing gets done, and it doesn't drive you crazy along the way.

This journal is going to help you to help yourself. I'll guide you through a series of exercises and techniques so that you can work out what you want and plot exactly how you're going to get it.

I call this

Winning at Life

(But not in the Charlie Sheen way. You don't need to be an insufferable prick about it.)

#WINNING

In my book—and in The Game of Life—you're competing exclusively against yourself. Not other players, not even the computer. Just you, clearing a path toward victory by getting your shit together and getting out of your own damn way.

How to use it

Think of this journal as your nifty little repository for tidying your metaphorical shit and organizing your life so you can spend more time on the things you truly give a fuck about—making your life easier and better along the way.

Like, a *lot* easier and better, no matter where you're starting from.

You may be literally lying on your couch, sitting at a bus stop or dangling your feet from the Herman Miller Aeron chair behind your big shiny desk—but I'm guessing you picked up the *Get Your Sh*t Together Journal* because, figuratively, you're in somewhat of a rut. And there's no shame in that.

Your rut could be shaped like a pair of red wine–stained comfy sweatpants. It might be lined with the silvery stock options that you stand to cash in, if you can just stick with your soul-killing job for five more years. Or maybe—and this is probably more likely—your rut takes the form of the usual daily grind: work, finances, family and friends, and a lot of other shit you need help staying on top of, plus neglected health (and even more neglected hobbies), finished off by the dreams you only admit to friends after a few cocktails ... or are too scared or anxious or overwhelmed to admit to yourself at all.

Sound familiar? Well then, strap in!

Oh, and grab a pen. You're gonna need it.

SMALL
SHIT

TOUGH
SHIT

DEEP
SHIT

I'm about to guide you through a series of practical exercises, flowcharts, and tools to help you organize your shit, set goals, and push through thorny obstacles to reach those goals. If that sounds like far too much of a commitment, don't worry: I'm not here to teach you how to do a million separate things—there isn't enough Purell in the world for that kind of hand-holding. I'm here to show you how to *approach* all the different stuff in your life so you can get it done in your own way, on your own schedule.

Basically, this journal will liberate you from the shit you think you SHOULD be doing, so you can bang out the shit you NEED to do and get started on the shit you WANT to do.

We'll go over:

Mental decluttering

The What/Why Method for
setting goals

Three simple tools for getting
(and keeping) your shit together

Time-management

The Power of Negative Thinking

Turning your to-do list into a
must-do list

Prioritizing and [responsible]
procrastination

And tons of other awesome shit!

Mental decluttering

Like decluttering your physical space, mental decluttering takes two forms. The first is DISCARDING. In my book *The Life-Changing Magic of Not Giving a Fuck,* I thoroughly explain this part. It involves sorting your time, energy, and money (aka your "fuck bucks") by things that bring you joy vs. things that *annoy,* then spending them on the former and doing away with the latter.

That's called making a Fuck Budget. Highly recommended.

But getting your shit together is all about ORGANIZING, and that's what this journal is for. It will help you deploy your time, energy, and money more efficiently—not only on things you *need* to do, but on those extra bonus-level things you *want* to do and just can't seem to afford or get around to. Big life changes, small life changes, whatever. They don't start with cleaning out the garage.

They start with
cleaning out
your mind.

SMALL
SHIT

Nailing down
the day-to-day
to build a
better future.

Winning at your life

This seems like a good time to ruminate on what constitutes winning at life. YOUR life. Use the next few pages to reflect on what results, emotional or material, would see you doing a victory lap like [a much, much slower and less spectacularly chiseled] Usain Bolt:

Remember, I'm not talking about what anyone else considers winning, or what goals and results you think you should *want. Just the things that honest-to-goodness make you happy.*

READY

SET

GOAL!

Now that you've resolved to get your shit together, the first thing you need to do is set some goals. If you don't know how to do that <waves to Theodore> then I've got a super-easy two-step plan of attack.

I call it the What/Why Method, and all it takes is asking yourself—and honestly answering—two questions, the answers to which will lead you to your goal.

Step 1:

what's wrong with my life?

Step 2:

why?

Your goal has to solve the problems set out in these two questions. So, for example:

1. What's wrong with my life?
   I hate my job.

2. Why?
I've been at the same place for ten years and the work doesn't interest me anymore.

3. Goal
Get a new job.

Setting realistic goals

Holding yourself up to an unreasonable standard is no way to win at life. It's OK to lower the bar a tad, especially when you're just starting out. For example, normal people who want to get fit aren't likely to wind up looking like Kate fucking Upton. Striving for that goal is like running toward a finish line that will always be moving farther and farther away, which is really discouraging. Instead, set realistic goals based on what annoys *you* about *your* life — not based on someone else's measurements — and begin the process of sweeping it out the damn door. Understanding and accepting what might be too far out of reach is not only completely OK, but essential to winning at life.

Give it a try.

WHAT'S WRONG WITH MY LIFE?

WHY?

GOAL

WHAT'S WRONG WITH MY LIFE?

....

....

....

....

WHY?

....

....

....

....

GOAL

....

....

....

....

WHAT'S WRONG WITH MY LIFE?

WHY?

GOAL

So you've set a few goals. Fabulous! Now what you need are the tools with which to achieve them. And I'm about to reveal how three little items from your everyday life hold the key to getting, and keeping, your shit together.

You may be surprised to learn they've been there all along.

Get Your Shit Together (GYST) Theory

There are 3 pillars to having your shit together, whether it's at work, home, or play.

Pillar 1: STRATEGIZE
Set a goal and make a plan to achieve that goal in a series of small, manageable chunks.

Pillar 2: FOCUS
Set aside time to complete each chunk.

Pillar 3: COMMIT
Do what you need to do, to check off your chunks.

Now, take out your keys,
phone, and wallet.

Getting your shit together—metaphorically speaking—is like keeping track of your keys, phone, and wallet. With each of these little things, you can do a bigger thing.

If you can manage to stay on top of those little life-management tools, you can use them to win at life.

Your keys are the ability to strategize—they unlock the next steps.

Your phone is the ability to focus—make those calls, mark that calendar.

Your wallet represents commitment—this is when you put your real or metaphorical money where your mouth is, to follow through on your plan.

GYST THEORY

$$Keys = Strategy$$
$$+ \qquad +$$
$$Phone = Focus$$
$$+ \qquad +$$
$$Wallet = Commitment$$

Shit + Together

Humans invented fire,
mapped the Arctic Circle
and created hologram Tupac.
We didn't do any of that shit
without a plan!

So start
making
that plan,
Stan!

The Power of Negative Thinking

There are many gurus out there for whom the word "aspirational" is a real turn-on. They want you to be the best version of yourself, work the hardest and reap the most reward. But a lot of people aspire to have and to do less, not more; a lot of us don't really know what happiness will look like for us, we just know we don't have it.

This is where the Power of Negative Thinking comes in. Instead of daydreaming about a theoretical future of being richer, thinner, or tidier, you focus on NOT being broke, fat, and messy in the here and now.

Goal-setting doesn't have to be about aspiring to what you want to be, so much as putting an end to what you *don't* want to be. By focusing on the negative, you can start finding your way toward the positive.

Goal #1

....

....

....

My strategy to achieve it:

....

....

....

....

....

....

....

....

....

....

....

Remember, break your overall plan down into small, manageable chunks. A strategy is simply all the small steps of a plan—your plan—neatly bundled on the key ring and ready to be put into action.

Goal #2

....

....

....

My strategy to achieve it:

....

....

....

....

....

....

....

....

....

....

....

Goal #3

....

....

....

My strategy to achieve it:

....

....

....

....

....

....

....

....

....

....

....

Now it's time

for a little

FOCUS POCUS.

Whip out that phone

In the twenty-first century, phones are basically magic. They do everything from making calls to taking pictures to spying on your nanny while you're at work. With this one little device, you can manage your entire life—work, dating, travel, banking—you name it, there's an app for it. But although you may have twenty-five apps running in the background and a monster to-do list, you can only *use* your phone to do one thing at a time. Skype with your parents. Reply to your boss's email. Book a flight. Lay down the greatest Instagram caption EVER.

And much has been written by more science-y people than me about the myth of multitasking but, suffice it to say, if you think you're watching your daughter's soccer game *and* composing a clever rejoinder to your office nemesis, then you're doing at least one of these things badly, probably both.

The same goes for getting your shit together. FOCUS. Small, manageable chunks. One. Thing. At. A. Time.

Give yourself the time and space to do the shit that needs doing.

By the way, calendars are tools for winning at life. Not using a calendar would be like playing Chutes and Ladders with no ladders. Get yourself a calendar. Go ahead, I'll wait.

What will you do each day to get you closer to your goals?

Day 1

Goal #1 action:

....

....

....

....

Goal #2 action:

....

....

....

....

Goal #3 action:

....

....

....

Day 2

Goal #1 action:

Goal #2 action:

Goal #3 action:

Day 3

Goal #1 action:

....

....

....

....

Goal #2 action:

....

....

....

....

Goal #3 action:

....

....

....

....

Day 4

Goal #1 action:

....

....

....

....

Goal #2 action:

....

....

....

....

Goal #3 action:

....

....

....

....

Day 5

Goal #1 action:

....

....

....

....

Goal #2 action:

....

....

....

....

Goal #3 action:

....

....

....

....

Day 6

Goal #1 action:

....

....

....

....

Goal #2 action:

....

....

....

....

Goal #3 action:

....

....

....

....

Day off!

It's important to reward yourself for a job well done. Make a list of fun shit you could do with your day off—and then DO IT.

....

....

....

....

....

....

....

....

....

....

....

Refer back to this page whenever you need fresh motivation for attacking that strategy.

Doodling page

Saying "I do."

If you want to get a new job (or throw a killer dinner party, run a five-minute mile, clean your house, or write a novel, for that matter), you have to COMMIT. You must put one real or metaphorical foot in front of the other. I liken this to taking out your real or metaphorical wallet and putting your real or metaphorical money where your mouth is. It's not only dollars that can represent action and commitment.

"But [thing I want to do] is too hard!"

Saddle up, cowboy, because I don't believe in "too hard." If you're going to argue with me on this you should probably stop reading now and go see if Barnes & Noble will refund your money on this journal. Or is it too hard to put on some trousers, get in your car, drive to the shop and admit to the assistant that you don't actually want to get your shit together?

I thought so.

As far as I'm concerned, there are only degrees of difficulty along an achievable continuum of goals. If you set a realistic goal with parameters within your control, it can be achieved.

For example, *I* think it would be "hard" to run a marathon, whereas I have several friends who seem to find completing a 26.2-mile road race easier than being on time for a dinner reservation. Yet people all over the world manage both of these tasks every day, so neither can be "too hard." I wouldn't set the marathon-running goal for myself but, if I did, it would theoretically be achievable.

In other words, "hard" is subjective, but "too hard" is just another way of saying "I quit before I even tried."

Whether you're an Alvin, a Simon, or a Theodore—you need to get in the zone and get your shit together.

WAYS TO GET
IN THE ZONE

Don your lucky underpants

•

Do five jumping jacks

•

Listen to the *Karate Kid* theme song

•

Light a scented candle

•

Pinch your cheeks to get
that healthy glow

WAYS I CAN
GET IN THE ZONE

....

....

....

....

....

....

....

....

....

Feeling
overwhelmed?

It's OK. Take time out. Mix yourself a cocktail. (That's what I just did, while compiling this journal.) If you're a teetotaler, bust out the Earl Grey. Remember that the overarching goal of getting your shit together is to make your life *easier,* not harder. And in an ideal world, it would be rather fun as well. So once you've got your hot toddy or hot tea, grab a few colored pencils and have a go at the next page. You can start now and come back to it whenever you need to give yourself a little break.

Life is like an adult coloring book. You simply work your way through each little section until the big picture materializes before you.

Understanding time

Once you know where to begin, it's time to think about *when*. You can set your clock by Theodores forgetting to set their clocks, but time-management can also be the Achilles' heel of the most competent Simons among us. Why is that? I mean, we're surrounded by time-telling devices in our homes, cars, offices, and everywhere else. Watches, iPhones, cable boxes, microwaves, Big Ben, sundials, THE SUN ITSELF.

These are built-in tools to help human beings manage time. Everyone should be using them! (Did you go out and buy that calendar yet?)

But for people who don't have their shit together, there never seems to be *enough* time. Too much on the to-do list, too few hours in the day—or so they claim.

Being perpetually late or having poor time-management skills boils down to one thing: not actually knowing how long it takes to do anything. If you have this problem—but you're ready to become a new, better, more reliable you—the first step in getting your shit together and being on time is to, well, time yourself.

Time flies when you don't

have your shit together.

Step 1: Time yourself doing daily tasks.

Step 2: Do this every day for a week.

Step 3: Crunch the numbers — get intimate with how much time your morning ablutions, finishing up at work or assembling your favorite midnight snack really takes.

Step 4: Voilà, now you understand how time applies to your life. Start using it for good, not evil.

Shit you could time yourself doing

Getting dressed in the morning

Commuting (or getting from any point A to any point B)

Working out

Balancing the books

Getting your kids out the door for school

Reading the paper cover to cover

Blow-drying your hair

Masturbating

Leaving the office

TASK _____

DAY	TIME	NOTES
Sunday	_____	_____
Monday	_____	_____
Tuesday	_____	_____
Wednesday	_____	_____
Thursday	_____	_____
Friday	_____	_____
Saturday	_____	_____

TASK _____

DAY	TIME	NOTES
Sunday	_____	_____
Monday	_____	_____
Tuesday	_____	_____
Wednesday	_____	_____
Thursday	_____	_____
Friday	_____	_____
Saturday	_____	_____

Now, I'm not asking you to shower faster or kick your kids out of the house without breakfast. The secret to time-management isn't speeding up or slowing down. It's about strategy and focus. Strategy: how much time does X take? Focus: if X is a necessary task, schedule Y minutes/hours to get it done; and/or undertake X task only when you have Y minutes/hours available. In other words, don't try to shove a square phone call with your mother into a round five minutes.

Time is the mothership from which two competing forces — prioritization and procrastination — descend to create order or wreak chaos in your life.

TASK _____

DAY	TIME	NOTES
Sunday	_____	_____
Monday	_____	_____
Tuesday	_____	_____
Wednesday	_____	_____
Thursday	_____	_____
Friday	_____	_____
Saturday	_____	_____

TASK _____

DAY	TIME	NOTES
Sunday	_____	_____
Monday	_____	_____
Tuesday	_____	_____
Wednesday	_____	_____
Thursday	_____	_____
Friday	_____	_____
Saturday	_____	_____

Fuck Overload™

Giving too many fucks—without enough time, energy, or money to devote to them—keeps you overbooked, overwhelmed, and overdrawn. This leads straight to Fuck Overload™, a state of anxiety, panic, and despair. Possibly tears. Despair, for sure. Why? Because even if you really need to give all of those fucks, you cannot give them all at once. That's where prioritizing comes in handy.

(And if you *don't* really need to give all of those fucks, well, I know a book that can help.)

A PRACTICAL PARODY

the life-changing
magic of **NOT GIVING A F*CK**

how to stop spending time you don't have
with people you don't like
doing things you don't want to do

sarah knight

Lists are a huge help in getting your shit together. If you're like me, you probably have a running to-do list as a catch-all for everything you know you have to do in the near future. Or maybe you just have forty-seven Post-it notes stuck to your laptop at all times. Either way, when your to-do list starts to resemble *War and Peace* and you're approaching Fuck Overload™, you need to PRIORITIZE. Not everything needs to truly, madly, deeply be done today, right?

So take that to-do list and shorten it into a *must-do* list.

The Must-Do Method

_____

1. Make a to-do list

2. Relist the items based on urgency

3. Move what has to get done today to a new, must-do list

4. Do that shit and save the rest for tomorrow

5. Repeat steps 1–4

ALL THE SHIT I HAVE TO DO

All the shit I have to do

All the shit I have to do,
in order of urgency

All the shit I MUST do today

done, done, and diggity-DONE ◯

Prioritizing takes you BEYOND the magic of not giving a fuck, into a land of ass-kicking and name-taking. Theodores will marvel at their newfound levels of productivity; Alvins will realize that life doesn't have to be such a slog; Simons will hone their natural capacity for efficiency and feel even more superior to their brothers than they already did.

Responsible procrastination: postponing actions that are low priority in order to turn your overwhelming to-do list into a manageable must-do list.

ALL THE SHIT I HAVE TO DO

All the shit I have to do

All the shit I have to do,
in order of urgency

All the shit I MUST do today

done, done, and diggity-DONE

ALL THE SHIT I HAVE TO DO

All the shit I have to do

All the shit I have to do,
in order of urgency

All the shit I MUST do today

done, done, and diggity-DONE ◯

ALL THE SHIT I HAVE TO DO

All the shit I have to do

All the shit I have to do,
in order of urgency

All the shit I MUST do today

done, done, and diggity-DONE ◯

Procrastination station

We've all been there. You're in the zone, your must-do list is on point, you've started a task and—suddenly—procrastination sets in. The best thing you can do for yourself is be aware of the problem. To that end, please write down all the things you did this week in order to put off the shit you really had to get done. The longer your list, the more emphatically this whole point gets made.

(In case you're wondering, I'm not immune to this behavior. I just hide it better than most people.)

Ten things I've done that weren't on my to-do list in order to procrastinate doing things that were

---

Cut my cuticles

Researched various skin conditions I might have

Watched *Ocean's Eleven* for the fiftieth time

Engaged in fruitless political debate on Facebook

Folded someone else's laundry

Conducted a Tabasco vs. Crystal hot sauce
blind taste test

Color-coded my ChapStick collection

Tried (and failed) to memorize the lyrics to
"Nuthin But a 'G' Thang"

Contemplated the divinity of Helen Mirren

Kegels

Good news!

Any time you're looking for a responsible way to procrastinate, you could do so by consulting this handy flowchart. It's simple and easy-to-follow, and even staring blankly at it is more productive than staring blankly at other things, such as walls or your cat.

GET YOUR SHIT TOGETHER

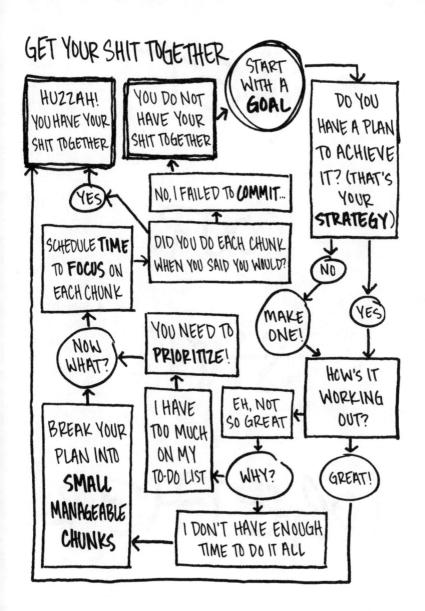

START WITH A **GOAL**

HUZZAH! YOU HAVE YOUR SHIT TOGETHER

YOU DO NOT HAVE YOUR SHIT TOGETHER

DO YOU HAVE A PLAN TO ACHIEVE IT? (THAT'S YOUR **STRATEGY**)

NO, I FAILED TO **COMMIT**...

YES

SCHEDULE **TIME** TO **FOCUS** ON EACH CHUNK

DID YOU DO EACH CHUNK WHEN YOU SAID YOU WOULD?

NO

MAKE ONE!

YES

NOW WHAT?

YOU NEED TO **PRIORITIZE**!

HOW'S IT WORKING OUT?

BREAK YOUR PLAN INTO **SMALL MANAGEABLE CHUNKS**

I HAVE TOO MUCH ON MY TO-DO LIST

EH, NOT SO GREAT

WHY?

GREAT!

I DON'T HAVE ENOUGH TIME TO DO IT ALL

GET

YOUR

SHIT

TOGETHER

AND GET
OUT OF
YOUR
OWN WAY

TOUGH
SHIT

The art of ~~war~~ willpower

Now, I can give you the motivational tricks and tips on time-management. I can simplify the steps and I can put a charmingly obscene twist on the self-help genre to keep your spirits up. But I can't inhabit your brain and body and *make* you follow my advice. If I could do that, I would have a reality show and a lip kit line by now.

Only you can get your shit together, set your goals and go forth and win at life — your life, whatever that involves. In order to stay committed to those goals, you're gonna need some willpower.

But it's only a little bit of willpower at a time! Enough to focus and complete those small, manageable chunks of your plan.

If you're motivated by:	Use this strategy:
Money	The Scrooge McDuck *Envisage yourself rolling around in piles of all that loot you're saving/not spending.*
Vanity	The Photo Finish *Taping a picture of your thinner self to the fridge isn't the* worst *way to shut down the Wizard of Impulse Control.*
Adulation	The Ego Boost *Life-winners are often admired by their peers. If that appeals to you, use it as fuel.*
Fear	The Power of Negative Thinking *Good for lighting a fire and keeping it hot.*
Accountability	The "Who Raised You?" *Gives you a swift kick, just like Mom used to.*

Who raised you?

Who raised you? is my second favorite thing to think/
mutter when I encounter someone making poor
life choices. And while I intend it sarcastically—as
though given their lack of self-control/hygiene/
manners they might have been brought up by a pair
of outlaw raccoons—it's actually a good question to
ask if you haven't had much luck being accountable
to *yourself* lately. If you have a hard time mustering
or sustaining willpower, you may be subconsciously
looking for someone else to thump it into you.

An emotional spanking, so to speak.

Saying "Who raised you?" helps you recognize the
behaviors that would cause your mother to say, "For
fuck's sake, get your shit together." (Which is, of
course, my favorite thing to think/mutter when I
encounter someone making poor life choices.)

If you wonder: *why can't I get a girl to spend the night, let alone develop a meaningful relationship with me?*

Ask yourself: *would my mom approve of the nest of dirty boxer shorts I've built on my bed in lieu of doing laundry? If not, why would* any *woman?*

If you wonder: *why is everyone getting promoted except me?*

Ask yourself: *what would my mom say if she knew I spent half the day on* Bachelorette *message boards instead of doing my job?*

If you wonder: *why can't I afford nice things?*

Ask yourself: *would my mom be proud to know that every month my salary gets spent almost exclusively on weed and Visine?*

A spoonful
of willpower
helps the medicine
go down.

Also: don't be such a fucking martyr

We all need a good whinge sometimes, but nobody needs to hear about how busy you are every hour of every fucking day. A pity party is a shitty party. And, more importantly, you should not *be* busy every hour of every day.

Having your shit together and winning at life is supposed to make you feel freer and looser, like your favorite tracksuit bottoms. It's not a competition—with yourself or anyone else—to be the most booked-up, burdened, and burned-out. I mean, look what happened to Joan of Arc. SHE WAS A MARTYR AND SHE WAS *LITERALLY* BURNED-OUT.

Strategize

Getting your shit together for the big
stuff is just getting your shit together for
a bunch of small stuff, over time.

Strategize

ALL THE SHIT I HAVE TO DO

All the shit I have to do

All the shit I have to do,
in order of urgency

All the shit I MUST do today

done, done, and diggity-DONE ◯

Focus

Do not go out for donuts.

Do not click on *TMZ*.

Do not check the box scores.

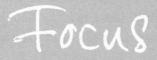

Distance yourself from distraction!

Like Arya Stark in *Game of Thrones,* distraction comes in many guises—and she is here to fuck your shit up. If focus is akin to the phone on which you schedule your life, distraction is like losing said phone. There are three ways to distance yourself from distraction:

- **Take evasive action**
  You know your own weaknesses, so don't let Arya exploit them. If you have a compulsive Twitter habit, don't keep the app open when you're trying to get shit done.

- **Stop, drop, and roll**
  If despite your best intentions you find yourself face-to-face with Twitter, treat the situation as though you are literally on fire. Stop scrolling, drop your hands to your sides and roll away from your device.

- **Pencil it in**
  There's no harm in taking a mental break every once in a while. A break only becomes a dangerous distraction when it's unplanned or goes on way too long. Schedule a ten-minute break for every hour of work, and enjoy!

Meet the Wizard of Impulse Control

If distraction is Arya Stark, then impulse control is more like the Wizard of Oz. This isn't some badass changeling assassin. Nope, just a man in a silly waistcoat pulling mental levers willy-nilly behind the curtain of your brain, causing trouble. He gets away with a lot when you refuse to look behind said curtain and reprimand him. Once you start paying attention, he'll have no choice but to fall in line.

Impulse control should not be confused with distraction, which comes at you from all sides, when you least expect it, and in many forms. It's hard to fight distraction because you can't control all of the *scenarios* in which it exists. That shit is sneaky. But impulses—to snack, to eat ice cream for breakfast, to stay snuggled in bed rather than sweating it out on the elliptical machine—those are all noted, processed, and acted upon (or not) by a single entity: YOU.

You haven't been "distracted" by a piece of cake.

You've acted on an impulse to slather gooey buttercream frosting on your tongue that, in the moment, was stronger than your desire to weigh less or be more fit. And there is nothing inherently wrong with that. But if acting on that impulse contributes to your feelings of anger, sadness, or frustration—to falling short of your goals—then you may need to admit you have a problem employee at the impulse control station, get your shit together and confront him head-on.

Hey, Wizard, cut that shit out!

●

I want to fit into the suit I bought for Greg's wedding, not eat that bag of peanut M&M's and then cry myself to sleep.

●

I'm excited about the tennis arms I'm currently developing, and I'll thank you not to impede my progress to the gym this morning.

●

How about you pull the lever for "Feelin' good about myself today" instead of the one for "Fuck, I did it again."

●

I'm on to you, buddy.

What are your worst impulses?

Get to know your biggest impulse triggers by keeping a list of them at hand, writing down how they make you feel and what they're stopping you from accomplishing. Then, the next time you feel the urge to give in to one, consult this list and RESIST.

Seems like it's about time for a

new set of goals . . .

Goal #1

....

....

....

My strategy to achieve it:

....

....

....

....

....

....

....

....

....

....

Remember: SMALL, MANAGEABLE CHUNKS!

Goal #2

My strategy to achieve it:

Goal #3

....

....

....

My strategy to achieve it:

....

....

....

....

....

....

....

....

....

....

What will you do each day to get you closer to your goals?

Day 1

Goal #1 action:

....

....

....

....

Goal #2 action:

....

....

....

....

Goal #3 action:

....

....

....

Day 2

Goal #1 action:

....

....

....

....

Goal #2 action:

....

....

....

....

Goal #3 action:

....

....

....

....

Day 3

Goal #1 action:

....

....

....

....

Goal #2 action:

....

....

....

....

Goal #3 action:

....

....

....

....

Day 4

Goal #1 action:

....

....

....

....

Goal #2 action:

....

....

....

....

Goal #3 action:

....

....

....

....

Day 5

Goal #1 action:

....

....

....

....

Goal #2 action:

....

....

....

....

Goal #3 action:

....

....

....

....

Day 6

Goal #1 action:

....

....

....

....

Goal #2 action:

....

....

....

....

Goal #3 action:

....

....

....

....

Day off!

You know what to do ...

"Me time"
is a right,
not a privilege.

You've got to lobby for your hobby

Let's take a break from all the shit that *needs* to get done, and start talking about the shit you simply *want* to do. Do you have a hard time justifying making time for such activities—aka "hobbies"—that seem to benefit no one but yourself?

Yes?

Well, fuck that shit!

Sacrificing your hobbies to the altar of the must-do list is no good. They should be ON the must-do list to begin with. Consider your hobbies—and the benefits you get from indulging in them—to be equally as important as the other stuff you "need" to do. Hobbies are not only an integral part of maintaining your happiness, they can go a long way toward balancing the annoyance of the more arduous, less-exciting must-do tasks on your list. You can think of time spent on a hobby as a reward for completing annoying time-and-energy-sucking shit.

A highly effective way to increase time spent on a hobby is to *let yourself* spend time on a hobby to *remind yourself* how much joy it brings.

Hobbies with which I have rewarded
myself for getting other shit done

Reading a book

Reading a trashy magazine

Sunbathing

Playing Words With Friends

Taking a bubble bath

What are some of your favorite hobbies?

Become pro-creation

Lots of people wish they could get their shit together to pursue not only hobbies, but specific creative goals—like writing, music, and art—but they're too bogged down in work, family commitments, or other obligations of the no-fun variety.

I get it.

It's not easy to "make time" for stuff that doesn't [yet or may never] pay the bills. But novels don't write themselves, guitars don't gently weep on command, and painting happy trees is not as easy as Bob Ross makes it look. At some point, you have to get your shit together in order to stop aspiring to do the thing and ACTUALLY DO THE THING, whether it pays the bills or just makes you happy.

The path to this version of life-winning is obstructed by two separate but related challenges. We'll call them the Scylla and Charybdis of getting your shit together.

(I know, I know. Bear with me. I can't pronounce their names either, but they were mythical sea monsters that flanked the one safe path through the Strait of Messina in Homer's *Odyssey*. Just focus on the sea monster imagery and you'll be fine.)

Scylla is SCHEDULING. If you work all day and have a busy family/social life—or are just so tired you keel over when you get home—when do you have time for creative stuff?

Answer: you have to *make* or *find* time.

By now, you probably expect me to trot out my trusty must-do list. And yeah, that's one way to tackle it, but its efficacy depends on the kind of creative person you are. A former colleague of mine worked on her novel very early in the morning before going to her day job. Apparently she was capable of producing quality words at this time every day—and committed to doing so regularly—because she ended up with a jillion-dollar book deal, and quit the day job.

A victory for must-do lists everywhere!

For others, the creative urge has to strike, and *then* you have to find time to exploit it. A melody might pop into your head during your morning commute, but you can't just bail on your 8:00 a.m. presentation because you suddenly found yourself in the groove. Still, you could take five minutes to jot down the basics of your inspiration and shuffle tomorrow's must-do list accordingly, to prioritize writing a new song. Not ideal, but it's a start. Scylla, you can work with.

This is where Charybdis comes in, which is THE MISTAKEN IDEA THAT THERE IS NO VALUE in the creative stuff you're trying to schedule.

Sailing safely around this salty sea-witch means accepting the notion that you may be devoting an hour—or several—every day or week to an activity that has no perfectly defined purpose, one that might result in a finished product or might not. Spending an afternoon painting in your room could be an extremely rewarding period of craft-honing that brings you a lot of joy even if it doesn't land you a gallery show. Then again, it might very well land you a gallery show just like it landed my former coworker a book deal. You'll never know until you try, will you?

Therefore, the best, most potentially winning path toward achieving your creative goals lies between FINDING TIME *and* GRANTING YOURSELF PERMISSION TO USE IT.

Tap dance right past Scylla and slip Charybdis a high-five on your way.

Do you have any creative goals? If so, what are they?

What are some concrete steps you could take to accomplish them?

"Selfish" is not a four-letter word

Making room for hobbies and creative goals is a prime example of my get-your-shit-together practice overlapping with my no-fucks-given philosophy. Yes, giving fewer, better fucks is an exercise in selfishness—focusing on what you *want* to do rather than what you *need* to do (or what *other people* think you *should* do). But there's nothing wrong with that! And this mindset serves you especially well in getting your shit together to pursue hobbies, creative work, or any other activity that doesn't necessarily "result" in anything other than you being happy.

Happiness is a goal in and of itself.

Remember all that stuff you wrote down on pages 28–9, about what constitutes "winning at your life?" Now that you've started getting your shit together, what kind of progress have you made?

Has anything changed? Have you discovered new ways to win? (Hint: such as prioritizing happiness as a goal in and of itself?) Update your list here:

GREAT.
I think you're
ready to tackle some

DEEP
SHIT.

Mental health,
existential crises,
and making
big life changes

Fuck perfect

No, seriously. Perfection is an illusion, a shimmering oasis in the desert of your mind. Holding perfection in your sights is a self-defeating strategy.

At a certain point, the time and energy you've poured into any of the items on your must-do list is going to reach critical mass, and the more of it you spend trying to get one thing perfectly perfect, the less time you have for any of the rest.

Suddenly, instead of having your shit together, your whole day has gone to shit.

But think about it this way: even the most-celebrated winners are rarely actually perfect. A competitive gymnast may be *aiming* for a fabled "perfect ten," but that almost never happens (especially with this new scoring system, which seems designed to drive little leotarded Simons to drink vodka shooters off the balance beam). And if one of those human pogo sticks can win an Olympic gold medal without being perfect, then you can certainly win at your own motherfucking life.

I'm telling you, kids, don't get hooked on perfection. It's no way to live.

Twelve steps for defeating perfectionism

1. Admit that, unlike the 1972 Miami Dolphins, you are powerless over perfection.
2. Believe that a power greater than you can help restore you to sanity.
3. Make a decision to turn your will over to the care of a lady who curses a lot.
4. Take a fearless inventory of your to-do list and then ruthlessly reduce it to a must-do list. Then go get some ice cream.
5. Confess to the exact nature of your perfectionism — but don't be *too* exact.
6. Be entirely ready to almost banish perfectionism from your life.
7. Humbly inquire of someone else whether you are, in fact, being ridiculous.
8. Make a list of all persons harmed by your perfectionist tendencies and be willing to apologize for being such a fucking stickler.
9. Make direct amends, except when you were totally right to be a stickler because otherwise your team never would have won the International Sand Sculpting Championships in Virginia Beach last year.
10. Continue to take inventory of your actions and make a mental note each time the world does not end because you failed to be perfect.
11. Improve your conscious understanding of giving fewer fucks and getting your shit together, referring as needed to the "bibles" in these fields.
12. Carry this message to other perfectionists; just don't be an insufferable prick about it.

Anxiety,
you ignorant slut.

Anxiety is like mental dust — it's largely invisible but always there, and the longer you ignore it, the more cloying and invasive it becomes. It covers all the REST of your clutter with a layer of extra shit, and seeps into the cracks and crevices, necessitating a slightly more finessed approach to mental decluttering.

(Alvins and Theodores have a little build-up in the corners, but Simons like me have been vacuuming this shit up and then inexplicably dumping the filter right back onto the floor our entire lives. It's a problem.)

Giving fewer fucks certainly goes some way toward solving this problem — you'd be amazed how many layers of anxiety-dust you can clear out when you stop caring about what other people think of your life choices. But you still have to *live* your life, and that means dealing with stuff that occasionally leaves you feeling like you're making out with a Roomba. What follows are simple approaches that could work for you:

Ripping off the Band-Aid

This is particularly useful in situations where you literally cannot move forward without taking action. For example, if getting your shit together means moving out on your roommates and into your own place where there are no takeout containers being used as ashtrays or guys named Clint buzzing at all hours, you may feel some anxiety about telling your bestie that you're breaking the lease, but you do *have* to tell her. You can't just pull a disappearing act in the middle of the night and you certainly can't pay double rent to maintain a second apartment just so you never have to have The Talk. Just do it. The anxiety you feel beforehand will be one thousand percent mitigated by the relief you feel afterward, in your smoke-free, Clint-free, one-bedroom.

This too shall pass

The opposite of the above approach, this is when you ignore the problem *juuuuuust* long enough that it resolves itself or goes away. I'm not talking full-scale avoidance, but a few deep breaths'-worth of prudent hesitation; maybe a day at most.

Say you get a cryptic email from your boss that sends you into panic mode. It's probably wise not to respond right away. Focus on something else for a while and it's entirely possible that with a little distance, you'll reread the message and it will reveal itself as totally innocuous. Or your boss will poke her head into your office and say something nice and you'll realize you were reading way too deeply into *Come see me when you have a second. Thanks.*

The Practice Test

Does anxiety sometimes manifest itself as having a never-ending conversation in your head instead of having that conversation with the real person who's causing you the anxiety? If so, and if it's not a conversation that *can* be had, I recommend getting it down on paper. This is a proven-to-be-effective therapeutic method and it's also fun to write sentences like *You are literally the worst person I've ever met in my life and, if I could, I would find out where you live, wait until winter, sneak into your house, and leave a McDonald's Filet-O-Fish sandwich tucked under your radiator. But since I don't have time for that shit, let me just say that what you did at Soul Cycle last Friday was unforgivable and you should be ashamed of yourself, Nancy.*

(If I predecease him, my husband has explicit instructions to burn my collection of notepads.)

The act of writing this stuff down helps release your anxiety into the void, and often prevents you from ever needing to *have* a real-life confrontation in the first place. So, what are you anxious about lately?

The other "F" words:

_____

FEAR

and

FAILURE

Fear

———

Real talk: not having your shit together is self-sabotage, pure and simple. You lost track of your keys, phone, and wallet? Great. You're locked out, blacked-out, and tapped out. Do the same with your metaphorical shit and you're likely to lose even more: opportunities, friends, respect, and the Game of Life altogether.

A lot of people let fear put them on the defensive. As a result, they lose sight of their goals and the path it takes to get there. Strategy flies out the window. The focus switches to "everyone else" instead of "me." And the only commitment they can muster is in making excuses for their behavior instead of changing it.

But in most cases? The world is not out to get you. YOU are out to get you. To paraphrase the Beastie Boys: you're scheming on a thing that's a mirage, and I'm trying to tell you now, it's self-sabotage.

What are you so afraid of?

List five of your greatest fears, and spend some time thinking about whether those fears are preventing you from getting your shit together. If they are, what can you do to counteract them?

Fear #1

....

....

....

....

....

Fear #2

....

....

....

....

....

Fear #3

....

....

....

....

....

Fear #4

....

....

....

....

....

Fear #5

....

....

....

....

Eventually the *fear* of failure becomes just as powerful and punishing as the failure itself, and it can be crippling. By being afraid of a potential bad outcome, you cause yourself even more agony surrounding the whole endeavor—whether it's passing a test, getting a promotion or correctly assembling any piece of IKEA furniture on the first try.

Failure

As Franklin Roosevelt once said, "The only thing we have to fear is fear itself." I would add unruly dogs, skydiving, and cancer to the mix, though I do not personally fear failure. But for everyone who does, I have to tell you: there are very few situations in which anyone is going to die on the table because you made the wrong decision. It doesn't have to be so fear-inducing.

When you accept that failure *is* an option, you move it from the realm of anxiety-inducing anticipation into a reality that you'll deal with when (and more importantly, IF) it ever happens. Your energy is better spent on accomplishing goals in the here and now than on worrying about failure in the abstract.

Failure is just a thing that happens. Sometimes you bring it on yourself, like when you decide to go to Burning Man without adequate sunscreen and Wet Wipes. Other times, it just sort of happens to you, like when you majored in Astronomy without knowing "Asteroid 4179 Toutatis" was going to collide with the planet on your watch. You can't win 'em all.

In other words: in order to get your shit together, you need to stop giving a fuck about failure. Which is an excellent use of f-words, if I do say so myself.

Things that are healthier
to fear than failure

Sharks

•

Bandits

•

Vampires

•

Scaffolding

•

Poisonous toads

•

Third nipples

Pitfalls in the Game of Life—such as poor time-management, distraction or fear of failure—are identifiable. The methods for counteracting or avoiding them are simple; by now, you should be able to STRATEGIZE like Garry Kasparov and FOCUS with one arm tied behind your back (you need the other one to hold your phone). The actual act of COMMITMENT is the hardest part, but when you want something badly enough, it's absolutely, positively, one hundred percent do-able if you have your shit together.

I know you are but what am I?

Here's a fun exercise taken straight from *Get Your Sh*t Together*. If you've done it already, you can skip the next few pages. (Go ahead and reward yourself for being ahead of the game by spending fifteen minutes indulging in a hobby—or a nap.) Anyway, before I wrote that book, I took a survey in which I asked respondents to "name something OTHER people do that makes you think they don't have their shit together."

So now I'm going to give you a list of complaints taken directly from my survey responses.

You're going to match each complaint with a person in your life who is guilty of this behavior.

And you're going to think about how *obvious* it is that they are engaging in self-sabotage to the nth degree, shake your head, mutter *Get your shit together* under your breath and keep going until you complete the list.

Have fun, I won't tell anyone.

_____ is really disorganized.

_____ is perennially late.

_____ says "that's just how I am," as though that's a valid excuse for always being late.

_____ can never seem to keep a promise.

_____ is in a bad relationship.

_____ is so irresponsible with money.

_____ always talks about starting a diet or workout program but never follows through.

_____ is so paralyzed by perfection, he/she never gets anything done.

_____ puts everything off until the last minute, then does a shitty job at it.

_____ is impossible to pin down/never commits to anything.

_____ is always spending money he/she doesn't have and is therefore always broke.

_____ complains about his/her job constantly but never looks for a new one.

_____ doesn't take care of him/herself and wonders why he/she feels gross all the time.

_____'s messy home is basically a reflection of his/her messy life.

_____ is so overcommitted, it would be comical if it weren't so sad.

_____ is terrible at responding to emails; it's like they go into a black hole.

_____ keeps doing the same thing over and over, expecting different results.

Now, you're going to stand in front of a mirror and instead of reciting your friend (or family member, colleague, neighbor, or acquaintance)'s name aloud, you're going to substitute YOUR OWN NAME.

Every time you experience a twinge of brutal recognition, that's self-awareness. Circle those answers. Meditate on them. Become the self-awareness you want to see in your friends/family/colleagues/neighbors/acquaintances.

Congratulations, _____, you just got one (or more) steps closer to winning at life.

GET

YOUR

SHIT

TOGETHER

AND START WINNING AT LIFE

TODAY'S DATE: _____

6 a.m.

7 a.m.

8 a.m.

9 a.m.

10 a.m.

11 a.m.

12 p.m.

1 p.m.

2 p.m.

3 p.m.

4 p.m.

5 p.m.

6 p.m.

7 p.m.

8 p.m.

9 p.m.

10 p.m.

11 p.m.

12 a.m.

Notes:

TODAY'S DATE: _____

6 a.m.

7 a.m.

8 a.m.

9 a.m.

10 a.m.

11 a.m.

12 p.m.

1 p.m.

2 p.m.

3 p.m.

4 p.m.

5 p.m.

6 p.m.

7 p.m.

8 p.m.

9 p.m.

10 p.m.

11 p.m.

12 a.m.

Notes:

TODAY'S DATE: ....

6 a.m.

7 a.m.

8 a.m.

9 a.m.

10 a.m.

11 a.m.

12 p.m.

1 p.m.

2 p.m.

3 p.m.

4 p.m.

5 p.m.

6 p.m.

7 p.m.

8 p.m.

9 p.m.

10 p.m.

11 p.m.

12 a.m.

Notes:

TODAY'S DATE: _____

6 a.m.

7 a.m.

8 a.m.

9 a.m.

10 a.m.

11 a.m.

12 p.m.

1 p.m.

2 p.m.

3 p.m.

4 p.m.

5 p.m.

6 p.m.

7 p.m.

8 p.m.

9 p.m.

10 p.m.

11 p.m.

12 a.m.

Notes:

TODAY'S DATE: _____

6 a.m.

7 a.m.

8 a.m.

9 a.m.

10 a.m.

11 a.m.

12 p.m.

1 p.m.

2 p.m.

3 p.m.

4 p.m.

5 p.m.

6 p.m.

7 p.m.

8 p.m.

9 p.m.

10 p.m.

11 p.m.

12 a.m.

Notes:

TODAY'S DATE: _____

6 a.m.

7 a.m.

8 a.m.

9 a.m.

10 a.m.

11 a.m.

12 p.m.

1 p.m.

2 p.m.

3 p.m.

4 p.m.

5 p.m.

6 p.m.

7 p.m.

8 p.m.

9 p.m.

10 p.m.

11 p.m.

12 a.m.

Notes:

TODAY'S DATE: _____

6 a.m.

7 a.m.

8 a.m.

9 a.m.

10 a.m.

11 a.m.

12 p.m.

1 p.m.

2 p.m.

3 p.m.

4 p.m.

5 p.m.

6 p.m.

7 p.m.

8 p.m.

9 p.m.

10 p.m.

11 p.m.

12 a.m.

Notes:

TODAY'S DATE: _____

6 a.m.

7 a.m.

8 a.m.

9 a.m.

10 a.m.

11 a.m.

12 p.m.

1 p.m.

2 p.m.

3 p.m.

4 p.m.

5 p.m.

6 p.m.

7 p.m.

8 p.m.

9 p.m.

10 p.m.

11 p.m.

12 a.m.

Notes:

TODAY'S DATE: _____

6 a.m.

7 a.m.

8 a.m.

9 a.m.

10 a.m.

11 a.m.

12 p.m.

1 p.m.

2 p.m.

3 p.m.

4 p.m.

5 p.m.

6 p.m.

7 p.m.

8 p.m.

9 p.m.

10 p.m.

11 p.m.

12 a.m.

Notes:

TODAY'S DATE: ....

6 a.m.

7 a.m.

8 a.m.

9 a.m.

10 a.m.

11 a.m.

12 p.m.

1 p.m.

2 p.m.

3 p.m.

4 p.m.

5 p.m.

6 p.m.

7 p.m.

8 p.m.

9 p.m.

10 p.m.

11 p.m.

12 a.m.

Notes:

TODAY'S DATE: _____

6 a.m.

7 a.m.

8 a.m.

9 a.m.

10 a.m.

11 a.m.

12 p.m.

1 p.m.

2 p.m.

3 p.m.

4 p.m.

5 p.m.

6 p.m.

7 p.m.

8 p.m.

9 p.m.

10 p.m.

11 p.m.

12 a.m.

Notes:

TODAY'S DATE: _____

6 a.m.

7 a.m.

8 a.m.

9 a.m.

10 a.m.

11 a.m.

12 p.m.

1 p.m.

2 p.m.

3 p.m.

4 p.m.

5 p.m.

6 p.m.

7 p.m.

8 p.m.

9 p.m.

10 p.m.

11 p.m.

12 a.m.

Notes:

Little, Brown and Company
Hachette Book Group
1290 Avenue of the Americas, New York, NY 10104
littlebrown.com

First North American Edition: August 2018
Originally published in Great Britain by Quercus Editions Ltd: June 2018

Little, Brown and Company is a division of Hachette Book Group, Inc.
The Little, Brown name and logo are trademarks of Hachette Book Group, Inc.

The publisher is not responsible for websites (or their content)
that are not owned by the publisher.

The Hachette Speakers Bureau provides a wide range of authors for speaking events.
To find out more, go to hachettespeakersbureau.com or call (866) 376-6591.

Some material previously published in *Get Your Sh*t Together* by Sarah Knight.

Illustrations and hand-lettering by Lauren Harms

Designed and typeset by Carrdesignstudio.com

ISBN 978-0-316-45154-3
LCCN 2018941035

10 9 8 7 6 5 4 3 2

LSC-C

Printed in the United States of America